OVER 150 GREAT PIZZA JOKES

by Phil Hirsch
and
Hope Honeyman

Illustrations by Jerry Zimmerman

DEDICATION

*For Joy, Kathy, Lee, and Charlie —
the "pie pipers" of Aventura, Fla.,
Bayside, N.Y., and Cherry Hill, N.J.
and Cory Evan Honeyman —
"You're the tops!"*

Published by The Trumpet Club
1540 Broadway, New York, New York 10036

ISBN 0-440-84426-6

*Printed in the United States of America
November 1992*

5   7   9   10   8   6   4
OPM

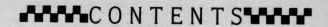

CONTENTS

RECIPE
FOR THE
PERFECT
PIZZA

When does a pizza lover go to Kentucky Fried Chicken?
When he or she is in a fowl mood!

What do baby doctors have in common with pizza store owners?
They both deliver!

Are pizzas wealthy?
Sure — they're rolling in dough.

Which popular singer was named after a pizza company?
Madonna-mo!

Who is the pizza's favorite relative?
Aunt Chovy.

How do we know army drill sergeants love pizza?
They keep shouting, "Pizza Hut, two, three, four!"

How did Italy honor the pie?
By building a monument — the
Tower of Pizza (Pisa).

Does pizza make people thirsty?
We drink so.

**What did the customer say when
the pizza baker told him, "I put
my heart into
that pie"?**
"Never mind your heart. How
about some pepperoni?"

**What did the pizza joint owner
say when the basketball team
called to say they were having a
pizza party?**
"That's a tall order!"

**Do you have to be strong to stay in the
pizza pie business?**
Sure — you must be a good boxer.

Which comic-strip hero adores pizza?
Pop-pie!

**What is the best kind of pizza party
to have?**
A surpies party!

How many pizzas does wrestling champ Hulk Hogan order at one time?
A piel of them.

How did the spaghetti get close to the pizza?
By using its noodle!

Why do golfers like pizza bagels?
They all want a hole in one.

How do reptiles order pizza pies?
Well, the croco dials!

**What do these reptiles prefer to drink
with their pizza?**
Gatorade!

**What did the food critic say about the
new pan pizza?**
What else? She panned it!

Why are pizzas round?
Who wants to be a square!

Are pizzas good show biz performers?
Of course — they're great at
entertainment!

Why do so many pizza parlor owners use Prudential Insurance?
They want a pizz-a the Rock!

What pizza personality is faster than a speeding bullet and able to leap over tall buildings in a single bound?
Supieman!

Why don't they make olive pizza?
It's the pits!

If you throw a pizza into two of the Great Lakes, how will it taste?
Erie, but Superior!

What happened to the guy who tried to throw a pizza into Lake Ontario and missed, and then tried to throw that pizza into another Great Lake?

Mished again (Michigan)!

What do you get if you throw a pizza into all five of the Great Lakes?

A wet pizza that doesn't wet (whet) your appetite!

What happened when the pizzeria owner substituted Swiss cheese for mozzarella on his pies?

It was a holey mess!

What happened when the pizzeria owner substituted cream cheese?

He got creamed!

Why are so many pizza parlors located in shopping centers?
Why not? The mall the merrier!

Why do pizzeria owners resent IRS agents eating in their stores?
IRS agents take too big a bite!

Why did Vanna White pour alphabet soup on her pizza?
To make it letter-perfect!

How can you get a job slicing pizza?
Who knows? But it's knife work if you can get it!

Why did the pizza write to Dear Abby?
Something must have been eating
at him!

**Why did the man eat in the same
pizzeria three times a day for nine
years?**
He hated his wife's cooking!

**Why won't pizzas sit in the front of
a restaurant?**
They prefer the pizza-rear!

Do pizzas do well in college?
Sure — many graduate Pie (Phi)
Beta Kappa!

What did the mama and papa pizza say to their child who wanted to be an astronaut?
"The pie's the limit!"

What happened to the first pizza to complete college?
It became the grad-u-ate!

When do dogs particularly like pizza?
When it's made with muttsarella cheese!

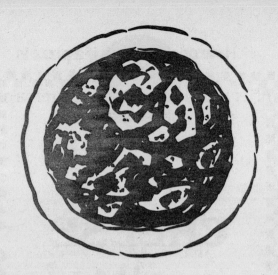

This is a drawing of:

1. A flying saucer
2. A lady's hat
3. The globe before Columbus set sail
4. A pie with everything on it
5. A finger painting by a child
6. None of the above

Why do young people like pizzas?
They're pro-teen!

How do you know if a pizza is left-handed?
After you're done eating, the remaining pieces are left!

Who discovered pizza?
The Pietalians (Italians).

If one slice costs $1 and eight slices cost $4, how much are sixteen and thirty-two?
Forty-eight.

What kind of books do pizzas like?
Spicy ones!

Are pizza store owners wealthy?
Sure — they make a lot of dough.

Can a pizza marry an octopus?
You must be squidding!

**How do you know if your pizza
can count?**

Ask it how much 6 minus 6 is, and if it
says nothing, you know it can count!

**Would you use spaghetti as a
pizza topping?**

Why not? It has pastabilities!

**Why did the pizza guy go out of
business even though his pizzas sold
like hotcakes?**

His customers wanted pizzas, not
hotcakes!

How do you spell pizza backwards?
P-I-Z-Z-A B-A-C-K-W-A-R-D-S.

Why don't pies do well in the ring?
Because you can easily box pizzas!

What happened to the man who claimed he ate a 30-foot pizza?
He had a bitemare!

Which historical leader was a great pizza eater?
Attila the Hun-gry!

Is the pizza in this restaurant worth talking about?
Talking about, yes; eating, no!

Did the knight's weapon come in handy to cut pizza?
Sword of!

Connect the dots and what do you have?

1. A pizza that bears watching
2. Time to enjoy pizza
3. A timeless pizza
4. A dialing (darling) of a pizza
5. A pizza whose time is up
6. All of the above

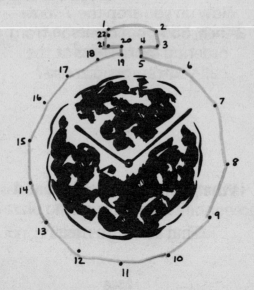

How do you stop the 7-foot-2-inch, 350-pound person from ordering more slices at the all-you-can-eat pizzeria?

You don't!

What do mathematicians and accountants say after eating pizza?

"That was sum meal!"

What's the best time to study pizza?
Lunchtime.

What happened to the pizza that was sent into orbit?
It became pie in the sky!

What term best describes a pizza baker during the 1960s?
A flour child!

Which subject in school is preferred by pizza lovers who order meatball, pepperoni, sausage, and salami toppings?
Arithmeatic!

**What happened at the Hawaiian hula
dance pizza party?**
It was Shake 'n Bake!

**What happened to the pizza dough
that was shipped north to
Juneau, Alaska?**
Don't Juneau?

**Seriously, what happened to the pizza
dough that was shipped north to
Juneau, Alaska?**
Wait, Alaska!

Who is the president of Pizza Land?
The Big Cheese!

STEP 4

BAKE THE PIZZA

What kind of person does a pizza want to avoid?

Anyone who bites off more than she can chew.

Why do pizzas love the Yuletide season?

There's pizza (peace) on earth.

Did Captain Hook like pizza?

Sure — he was a pierate!

In what battle did General Curtis die while eating pizza?

His last battle!

Why was the pizza made with red onions?
They ran out of white ones!

What penalty do football players risk when they go to a pizza parlor?
Pieling on.

Where do pizzas like to vacation?
In Florida — so they can bake.

**Why would someone go into the
pizza business?**
To make some dough!

What happened when the pizza married the frozen waffle?
They couldn't cut it!

Why are pizzas better than frankfurters?
Because hot dogs are the wurst!

Where do pizza parlor owners sign their important papers?
At the bottom, silly!

Is pizza a fast food?
Yes — you can eat it on the run!

When would a vampire find time to eat pizza?
During a coffin break!

How much did the man who baked a 27-foot pizza have to eat to get into the *Guinness Book of Records*?
The whole 9 yards.

What do pizzas sing as they go into the oven?
"Home, home on the range..."!

Do fine restaurants serve pizzas?
Only if they wear jackets and ties!

Why do pizzas hate turkeys?
They're gobblers!

Why else do pizzas hate turkeys?
They're fowl!

**What did the pizza parlor owner say
to his cook when he couldn't make
a pan pizza?**
Don't *pan*ic!

**What did the insurance agent tell the
baker when a huge pie fell on her?**
"Don't worry — you're covered."

EAT THE
PIZZA

**What will we celebrate when pizza
is 200 years old?**
Its piecentennial (bicentennial)!

**How can you tell when there are
2,000 pizza pies under your bed?**
You're much closer to the ceiling.

**Should you eat pizza with a knife
and fork?**
Well, a knife and fork are hard to digest!

Why did the pizza wear red suspenders?
The green ones broke.

Seriously, why did the pizza wear red suspenders?
To hold up his pants, of course.

THE BAD NEWS:
A monster pizza is invading your city.

THE GOOD NEWS:
It doesn't eat you — you eat it!

Why do pizza bakers enjoy their work?
They're doughing what comes naturally!

If you stacked 3,000 pizzas in your cupboard, what would you have?
A very large cupboard!

Why did the pizza visit Italy's capital city?
Be it ever so humble (pie), there's no place like Rome!

What music do pizzas fall asleep to?
Lullapies.

Which is a pizza's favorite expression?
"The pie's the limit!"

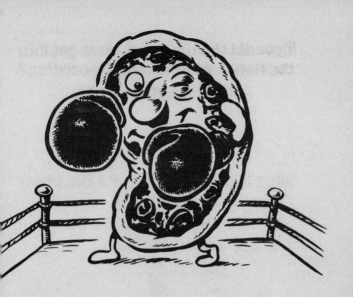

Do pizzas ever enter the boxing ring?
Sure — pizza's been a round.

What's the busiest day at pizzerias?
Chewsday!

What happened when the deep-dish pizzas went crazy?
It was *pan*demonium.

How did the thin-crust pizza get into the National Basketball Association?
It lied about its height.

What is the pizza's favorite Broadway show tune?
"There's No Business Like Dough (Show) Business"!

Can anyone improve on pizza as a food?
How can anybody improve on piefection?

What did the pizza eater do to the man who told him he hadn't had a bite in days?
He bit him!

Can you name three popular pizza toppings?
Why? They already have names.

Knock! Knock!
Who's there?
Pizza.
Pizza who?
Pizza nicer name than Joe!

Which pizza does the octopus like?
Octopie!

What do you have to be to spend your life making pies?
Oven lovin'!

In a pizzeria, if two's company and three's a crowd, what are four and five?
Nine.

Would you date a pizza?
Why not? They're hot stuff!

How does someone become a pizzeria owner?
Well, bakers can't be choosers!

What time is it when you've eaten a large pizza by yourself?
Time to stop eating.

Are pizzas good patients?
Sure — they're accustomed to high temperatures.

Do Italians hate pizza?
Don't be Si-silly (Sicily)!

STEP 6

LET THE PIZZA COOL

Ooops! Slight error. (Warning: In the future Step #6 should precede Step #5.)

**Why did the girl insist that she eat
pizza on the roof?**
She heard the meal was "on the house."

**Why didn't the pizzeria owner
pay taxes?**
He felt that making pies was taxing
enough!

**What's the difference between a 6-inch
and a 10-inch pizza pie?**
Around 4 inches!

Does ice cream go well with pizza?
Sure — haven't you heard of pie
a la mode?

To what reading club do pizzas belong?
The Book-of-the-Munch Club.

What can you say about most illegal pizza parlors?
They deliver hot goods.

How do you make a pizza green?
Mix a yellow pizza with a blue one.

Do baseball players like pizza?
Sure — they love to step up to the plate.

Can a pizza keep a job?
No. It always gets fired.

**Did you hear about the woman who
ate twelve pizzas a day for six months
and didn't gain a pound?**
Yes. She gained 18 pounds.

Why did the boy want to marry the pizza baker's daughter?
For her father's dough.

Why did the pizza quit school?
It thought life would be easy as pie!

Why did the pizza jump off the Empire State Building?
It wanted to see the stuff it was made of.

Why do undertakers eat pizza?
Because it rests in pieces.

How is pizza served in a restaurant?
At a table — like everyone else.

What were the first words of pizza's inventor, chef Aldo Pastori?
"Goo-goo, ga-ga."

What was the pizza doing at the Indianapolis Speedway?
About 200 miles per hour!

Do pizzas taste good with shrimps?
Sure — they can be eaten with people
of all sizes.

**Why did the lawyer refuse to accept
the crooked pizza as a client?**
He was too hot to handle!

Do you eat pizza with your fingers?
No. Pizza should be eaten with onion,
cheese, garlic, sausage, or pepperoni.

What instrument do pizzas prefer to play?
The pieano!

Answers to the classic line:
"Waiter, there's a fly in my pie."

"Shh, the other customers will want one, too."

"We don't charge extra!"

"Don't complain — it's better than half a fly!"

"I know. Watch him dive for the salami!"

"That's all right — he doesn't eat too much."

"Wait until you see what we put in the ice cream!"

"Hmm, there were two of them when I left the kitchen!"

"Should I have served him separately?"

"Oh, you wanted the mushroom pie?"

How do you find a pizza that's lost in the woods?

Go into the forest and make a noise like an anchovy.

Why did the pizza finally win its case in court?

Because pizza is so appealing!

What's the best remedy for a shirt stained by pizza?

A very long beard.

How do you make a pizza blue?

Tell it a sad story.

Why did the pizza delivery man carry a ladder?
He was delivering to a high school.

If you spill a bottle of soda on a pizza, what will it become?
Wet!

What kind of pie did the sculptor create?
Pie a la mold!

Why don't pizzas go to school?
They're in a class by themselves.

What did the pizza do when it was delivered to the rest room?
It took a nap!

What is the pizza's favorite TV program?
"Enterstainment Tonight" with Mary Heartburn.

"Lady, you've got a pizza on your head."
"What did you say?"
**"I said, 'You've got a pizza on
your head.'"**
"Oh, I must have eaten my hat
for lunch!"

**What did the pizza say when it was
wrapped in tin foil for the second
night in a row?**
"Curses — foiled again!"

**Which expression is a pizza parlor
favorite?**
"Dough unto others as you would have
others dough unto you."

What makes the Tower of Pizza lean?
It's on a strict diet!

What can be said about all pizzas?
They're well-bread!

When do old pizza eaters stop?
At red lights.

Should you eat pizza on an empty stomach?

No. A plate is better.

What happened when the pizza married the flounder?

Everyone thought something was fishy.

Did the pizza have fights with the flounder?

No. A pizza wouldn't hurt a sole!

What expression best describes the man who ate six pizzas a day?

Well-rounded.

How does a monster eat pizza?
By goblin' it!

What can you say about pizzeria waitresses?
They really know how to dish it out.

Where do you usually find pizzas?
Where you left them.

Why shouldn't the heavyweight champ fight the pizza pie?
He might get gar*licked!*

Do pizzas fall in love?
Sure — it's usually love at first bite.

The End
It's been slice knowing you!